S0-AHC-399

Published by Creative Paperbacks
P.O. Box 227, Mankato, Minnesota 56002
Creative Paperbacks is an imprint of
The Creative Company
www.thecreativecompany.us

Design and production by The Design Lab
Art direction by Rita Marshall
Printed by Corporate Graphics in the
United States of America

Photographs by Alamy (Nature Picture Library,
Andy Rouse-Wildlife), Dreamstime (Ryszard), Getty
Images (Jeremy Woodhouse), iStockphoto (Alarifoto,
Steven Cooper, Jonathan Heger, Eric Isselée, Holly
Kuckera, Frank Leung, Tommy Martin, Christian
Nasca, Nico Smit)

Copyright © 2012 Creative Paperbacks
International copyright reserved in all countries.
No part of this book may be reproduced in any
form without written permission from the publisher.

The Library of Congress has cataloged the hardcover
edition as follows:
Riggs, Kate.
Eagles / by Kate Riggs.
p. cm. — (Amazing animals)
Summary: A basic exploration of the appearance,
behavior, and habitat of eagles, Earth's most wide-
spread birds of prey. Also included is a story from
folklore explaining why people respect eagles.
Includes bibliographical references and index.
ISBN 978-1-60818-106-3 (hardcover)
ISBN 978-0-89812-691-4 (pbk)
1. Eagles—Juvenile literature. I. Title. II. Series.
QL696.F32R54 2012
598.9'42—dc22   2010049119

CPSIA: 030111 PO1446

First Edition
9 8 7 6 5 4 3 2 1

EAGLES

BY KATE RIGGS

CREATIVE
PAPER BACKS

Bald eagles (left) live in America, and tawny eagles (opposite) live in Africa

An eagle is a **bird of prey** called a raptor. There are 59 kinds of eagle. Eagles live on every **continent** except Antarctica. It is too cold for eagles to live there.

bird of prey a bird that hunts and eats other animals

continent one of Earth's seven big pieces of land

Eagles have wings and feathers, like other birds. Their beaks are curved, and they have sharp claws called talons. Most eagles are brown, black, or gray.

An adult eagle has about 7,200 feathers

Steller's sea eagles are some of the heaviest eagles. They weigh about 20 pounds (9 kg). Booted eagles are the lightest eagles. They weigh only about two pounds (0.9 kg). Harpy eagles are fast fliers. They can fly up to 50 miles (81 km) per hour.

Harpy eagles are the largest eagles in the Americas

Steller's sea eagles live on the coast of northeastern Russia

The 59 kinds of eagle can be divided into 4 groups. Sea eagles live near rivers, lakes, and oceans. Serpent eagles live in Africa, Asia, and southern Europe. Giant rainforest eagles live in hot, wet places around the world. And booted eagles live in many different **habitats**, from hot places to cold.

habitats places where animals live

An eagle grips a perch or prey with its talons

All eagles eat meat. They catch **prey** using their sharp talons and beaks. Fish and turtles are some of their favorite food. So are small animals such as mice, rabbits, and snakes.

prey animals that are killed and eaten by other animals

Mother eagles lay their eggs in a nest. Thirty to 60 days later, **eaglets** are born. Eaglets are covered with soft feathers called down. They leave the nest when they are four to five months old. Most eagles can live for 30 years in the wild.

eaglets baby eagles

Eagles usually live alone. They fly from place to place, looking for prey. Sometimes they eat animals that are already dead. The meat of dead animals is called carrion.

The bateleur (bat-eh-LOOR)
sometimes eats carrion

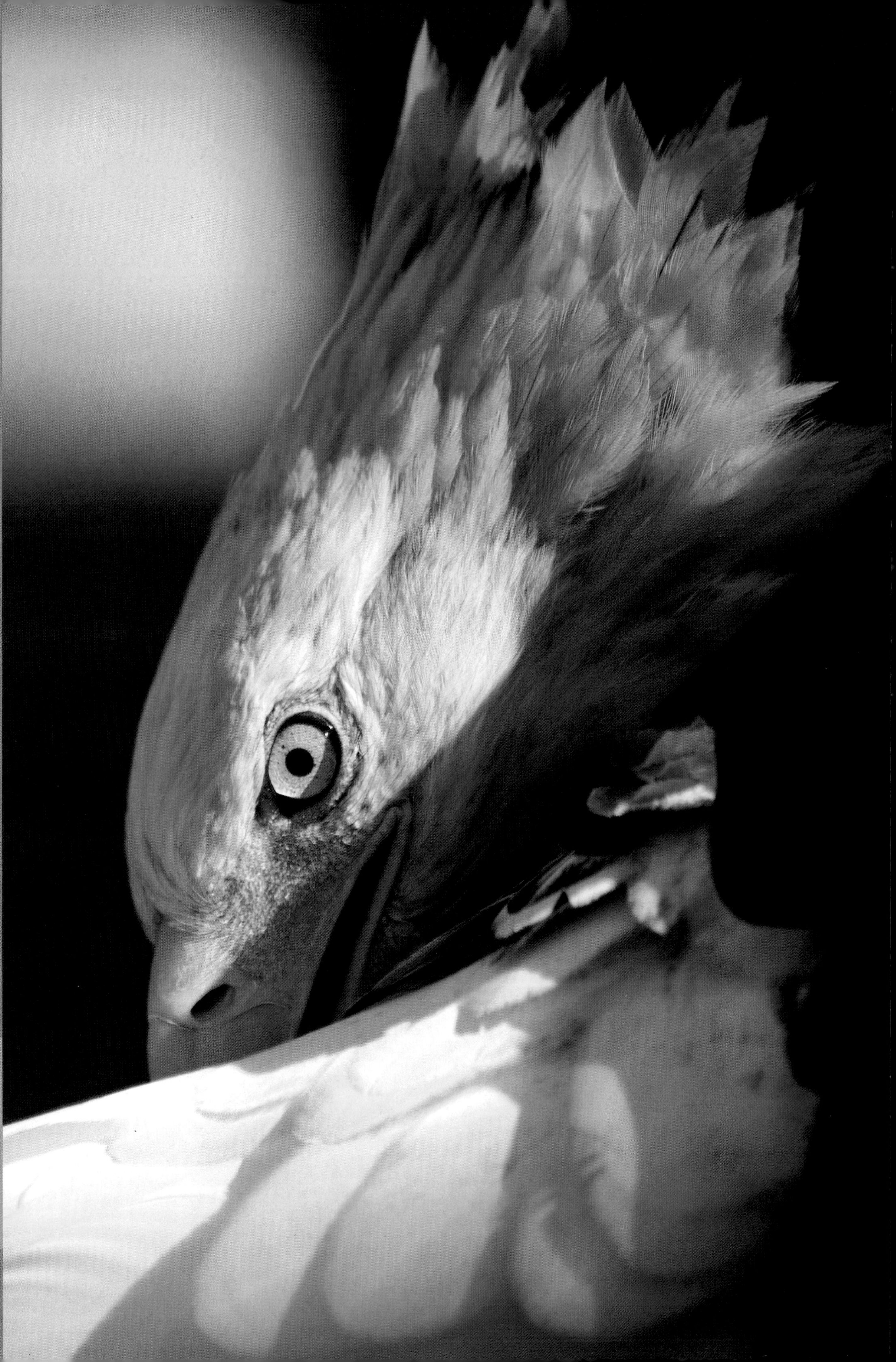

Sometimes eagles have to fly far away to find food. Then they rest in a nest or on a perch. Eagles use their beaks to clean their feathers a lot. This is called preening.

An eagle's feathers grow out of its skin, like human hair

People can see eagles flying over a river or sitting in a tree. Other times, eagles may be hunting prey and swooping close to the ground. It is exciting to watch these graceful birds fly!

An eagle keeps its toes curled up as it flies

An Eagle Story

Why do people respect the eagle? American Indians in the northwestern United States used to tell a story about this. Once, there was a great storm, and all the fish that lived in the waters near a village disappeared. The people were hungry. So a boy asked the eagles for help. The eagles liked the kind boy, so they brought the people all the fish they could eat. From then on, eagles and people respected each other.

Read More

Gibbons, Gail. *Soaring with the Wind: The Bald Eagle*. New York: HarperCollins, 1998.

Parry-Jones, Jemima. *Eagle & Birds of Prey*. New York: DK Publishing, 2000.

Web Sites

Enchanted Learning: Eagles
http://www.enchantedlearning.com/subjects/birds/printouts/Eaglecoloring.shtml
This site has eagle facts and a picture to color.

National Geographic Kids Creature Feature: Bald Eagles
http://kids.nationalgeographic.com/kids/animals/creaturefeature/baldeagle/
This site has pictures and videos of bald eagles.